ONE-PATCH PLUS

A New Twist on One-Patch Piecing

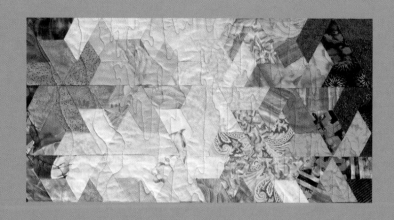

Louisa L. Smith

Lisa Harris

Quilt Escapes, LLC 4821 14th Street SW, Loveland, Colorado 80537
www.quiltescapes.com

Teachers:
Quilt Escapes, LLC encourages the use of this book as a text for teaching this procedure.

For more information contact:
Quilt Escapes, LLC
4821 14th Street SW
Loveland, CO 80537
970-593-1265
Or log on to: www.quiltescapes.com.

Library Of Congress Cataloging-In-Publication Data

Louisa Smith & Lisa Harris

One Patch-Plus, A New Twist On One-Patch Piecing / Louisa L. Smith and Lisa Harris.

ISBN 978-0-9795295-0-4

Published by Quilt Escapes, LLC
4821 14th Street SW
Loveland, CO 80537

Printed in USA

10 9 8 7 6 5 4 3 2 1

This book is dedicated to my daughter, Lisa a talented professional artist, for her continued support and encouragement to study color over the past 20 years.

This book is dedicated to my Mom, Louisa, who inspired my creative side and taught me how to sew. Also to my husband Brian who supported me during this endeavor.

Text © 2008 Louisa L. Smith and Lisa Harris

Artwork © 2008 Quilt Escapes, LLC

Photography: Rodney Stewart, unless otherwise noted.

Design/Illustration: Lisa Harris

Editor: Jean B. Hall

Copy Editor: Peg Chandler

Published by: Quilt Escapes, LLC

Front cover: ***Sandhill Cranes of Nebraska***
by Louisa L. Smith

CONTENTS

As a mother and daughter team, Louisa and Lisa share a love of quilting. For many years, Louisa has been teaching One-Patch Plus classes, and it is at the encouragement of her students that she decided to write this book. Utilizing Louisa's teaching and writing experience, along with Lisa's graphic design skills, the two decided to collaborate to bring you this book.

Their fascination with the one-patch is a long-standing one. Louisa has spent many rewarding hours making these easy, colorful quilts. And the appreciative comments received from others has made her realize that they too enjoy their efforts.

Louisa Smith

Patchwork Vest (curved diamond)
Louisa Smith, Loveland, CO 2008

Sandhill Cranes of Nebraska (curved kite) 64 ½" x 66 ½"
Louisa Smith, Loveland, CO 2005

To make your one-patch project as easy as possible, the creative process is broken into three major steps: Color, Design, and Theme. You will find the instructions simple to follow, no matter what your skill level. We hope they will help you create many wonderful quilts, using many, many fabrics.

One-patch quilts are based on traditional patterns, but they also offer many exciting contemporary design possibilities. Our goal is to help quilters of all abilities expand their horizons—and give them the courage to color outside the lines!

Supplies You'll Need

☐ **A color source.** Choose a photograph, image from a magazine, or piece of fabric with colors that are particularly pleasing to you.

☐ **A template** for the shape you have chosen. You can either make this yourself or purchase it from a manufacturer* or quilt shop.

☐ **A turntable** (optional), such as the Brooklyn Revolver,* for cutting small shapes.

☐ **A design wall.** If you already have a design wall in your workroom, that's great. If not, simply attach a flannel-backed tablecloth to an available wall.

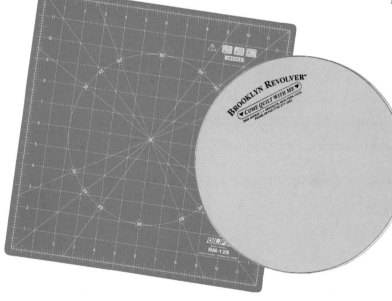

☐ **Fabrics for embellishing.** Look for prints of fish, flowers, or other shapes that reflect your theme.

☐ **Other embellishments.** Consider beads, ribbons, stamps, paints; plus any tool, product, or found object that will help create more interest.

☐ **Iron-on adhesive products** such as Wonder Under or Steam-A-Seam II, to attach appliquéed embellishments.

☐ **Threads for piecing and quilting.** Also consider specialty threads like Sulky® for embellishing with machine appliqué, needle painting, and quilting. Check out the "Blendables" by Sulky.®

☐ **Batting.** For hand quilting, I prefer thin and easy-to-needle battings such as cotton, silk or wool. For machine quilting, I recommend cotton batting, I recommend the Select Weight of Quilter's Dream Cotton,* a personal favorite or Warm & Natural.*

☐ **Fabrics for your top.** Collect small amounts of many fabrics in lots of colors, gradations, textures, and prints that reflect the colors in your source. The more, the merrier!

* See Resources.

Antique quilts have a character and charm all their own. And the antique quilts I find myself most often attracted to are the "one patches"—those entirely constructed using a single shape.

This shape can be as basic as a square, triangle, diamond, or hexagon. But there are also more unusual one-patch designs, such as the half clamshell, the curved kite, and the curved diamond.

Sometimes these designs are referred to as "tessellations"—mosaic-like patterns made-up of one (or sometimes more) shapes that completely cover a surface without any gaps or overlaps.

The one-patch has a long and interesting history. At the beginning of the 1800's, these quilts were popular because only small pieces of fabric were required, so a utilitarian quilt could easily be made from the remnants of old clothing.

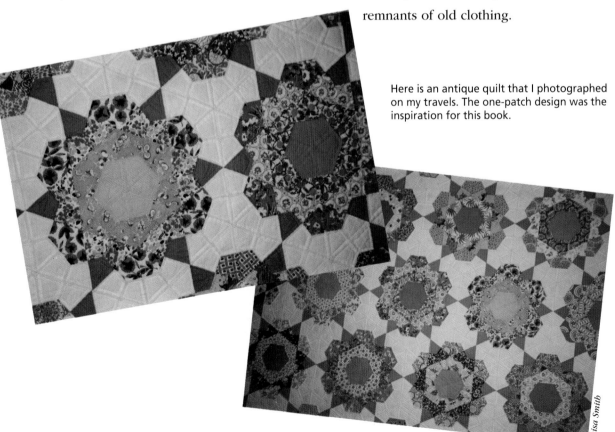

Here is an antique quilt that I photographed on my travels. The one-patch design was the inspiration for this book.

Louisa Smith

Out of Africa (curved diamond) 37 ½" x 54 ½"
Lee Ann Hopson, Cheyenne, WY 2006 Quilted by Laurie Sheeley

Later, in the Victorian era, upper-class ladies, who, unlike their less well-to-do sisters, could afford all the new fabric their hearts desired, made one-patches of luscious chintzes.

Nearing the end of the 19th century, "charm quilts," where no two patches were of the same material, were all the rage. In fact, trading fabrics became a popular pastime among fashionable young misses and matrons of the day, and manufacturers were deluged with requests for "samples" that would never result in larger orders.

The charm quilts of this period were usually constructed entirely out of silk. And while results were often spectacular, in all too many instances they were not long-lasting, as the silk tended to "shatter" into shreds as the decades passed. Still, a number of exceptional examples survive for our enjoyment.

The one-patch resurfaced in Depression-era quilts, primarily because of the recycling opportunities it presented to creative women with severely strained household budgets.

From the early to mid-1900's, one-patches also showed up in national quilt shows, where they often won grand prizes. Their popularity was due in part to their precision piecing, but mostly to the incredible variety of fabrics they contained. Judges were impressed by the number of pieces which was often proudly stated

on the entry form. It was not unusual for a prize-winning "postage stamp" quilt or other blue-ribbon one-patch to have 36,000 to 58,000 pieces!

When I started quilting in the late 1970s, I was fascinated by the popularity of scrap quilts. And I realized one of the big reasons my fellow quilters and I were so attracted to them was that you could use all the cotton fabric in your scrap bag regardless of color or design and never have to worry about running out of a particular fabric.

Around the turn of this century, one-patch charm quilts again became the focus of considerable attention—this time as "millennium quilts." To commemorate the year 2000, they were made from a minimum of 2,000 fabrics, each one used only once.

Quilters were trying very hard to incorporate at least a couple of fabrics specially printed for this once-in-a-lifetime event.

Most of these millennium quilts were constructed with absolutely no regard to color or pattern, and thus fall into the scrap quilt category.

In the early 1980s, I began my **One-Patch Plus** journey. The technique I developed, however, was anything but scrappy. I preferred to make the color sing and become the most important part of the quilt.

The first block I ever pieced was the Drunkards Path—not surprising considering my fondness for curves. Most of the shapes I have used in this and my other books are also curvy, with many of them also employing strip piecing.

That said, let's set off on our one-patch adventure by exploring some simple shapes, some strip piecing, and lots of curves.

We'll start by breaking the creative process into three easy steps: identifying sources for pleasing color combinations; choosing and manipulating the shapes you will use in your project; and picking a theme for your quilt, and selecting embellishments to enhance it.

This three-step approach lets you create wonderful, original pieces of fiber art, regardless of whether you are a beginner or an advanced quilter. And happily, you can get most of the raw material right from your stash, and use up lots of small bits you might otherwise throw away or consign to the attic.

All of which is why my students have christened me The Stash Buster—a name I wear with pride!

Chapter 2:
PICKING YOUR COLORS

Choosing the right colors for your one-patch quilt can be easy. The secret is to find a color source—a photograph, magazine picture, or piece of fabric that especially appeals to you—and analyze the colors it contains.

I usually pick an outdoor scene, because Mother Nature has a master's degree in color. And if you're like me (and most other quilters I know) you've probably already tucked away quite a few of these images that inspire you; why not dig one out that you've been saving because the colors just seem to talk to you?

Collecting fabrics is the next important step in the one-patch creative process. After all, even the best artist can't create a masterpiece without the proper

Melody Randol

Northern Exposure (kite) 44" x 71"
Louisa L. Smith, Loveland, Colorado 1999

paints! So once you've selected your color source, use it as a guide to check your personal stash for possibilities, and then take it to your favorite quilt shop to refer to as you consider additional purchases.

Start by picking out every fabric that even remotely resembles the colors in your source. (To figure out how to do this, it may help to examine the matched pairs of color sources and the quilts included in this book.)

Try to select not only the exact colors you see in your picture, but also some lighter and darker shades. You will need many, many fabrics in lots of gradations, the more the merrier! Light value fabrics are sometimes hard to come by, but remember that the back side of a fabric can be used as well, so you may be able to use both sides in the same quilt.

Besides lots of colors, you will need lots of textures and patterns too. Anything goes: plaids, dots, geometrics, and flowers. What's important is to have the right color; what the fabric depicts doesn't matter much. Even if it's covered with cats or hats or bats, if it has the colors you're after, it's the fabric you want.

You'll also discover that multi-colored fabrics are better for your purposes than tone-on-tone material. (If you're familiar with the **Strips 'n Curves** quilts in my

previous book, you already understand the importance of using gradations of many colors. The same principles apply to the one-patch quilts you will be creating.)

Take a moment now to look at the picture of the winter scene below that was the source for the **Northern Exposure** quilt also shown here. Look closely, and you will see that a wide variety of colors are included, even though the overall quilt looks almost monochromatic.

Why do additional colors in your fabrics make the total effect more satisfying? To explain, let me tell you a short story…

Many years ago, a friend of mine took a course from the famous artist Wayne Thiebaud at Cornell University. The first class assignment was to paint a dollar bill.

Now, you might think this kind of subject would be hard to draw but easy to select colors for. Just green and white, right?

Not so! Before he sent his students off to their brushes and palettes, Thiebaud instructed them to look very carefully at the colors of the bill before trying to duplicate them; to squint and try to see the touches of other colors that helped make up the whole.

In painting her dollar bill, my friend found she had to add bits of blue, yellow, black, white, and even red to her basic green. But the finished product was so realistic that when she hung it up in her dorm room, someone asked her why she had a dollar bill on her wall.

Lone Rancher (kite) 61″ x 43″
Lisa Harris, Johnstown, Colorado 2007

The point is, you don't get the realistic colors you see in nature from a tube. The sky isn't cobalt blue. The grass isn't veridian. A rose isn't cadmium red. And you can't create them with tone-on-tone fabric either.

It's the colors within the color—the endless minute gradations of hue, tone, and shade that make our world sparkle, and will make your quilts sparkle too.

So how do you keep track of all the fabrics you've collected while you're looking for more that coordinate; all the while designing your quilt? I do it by collecting small snippets of each piece stapling them to an 8 ½ by 11-inch piece of paper. That way, I have

Source image for **Lone Rancher** quilt.

something handy to consult while shopping and even more importantly, a pretty good idea of how my finished quilt will look. I refer to this as my "mock-up."

Source image for
Laconia Sunset quilt.

Laconia Sunset (isosceles triangle) 56" x 44"
Cathy Andrew, Westwood, Massachusetts 1998

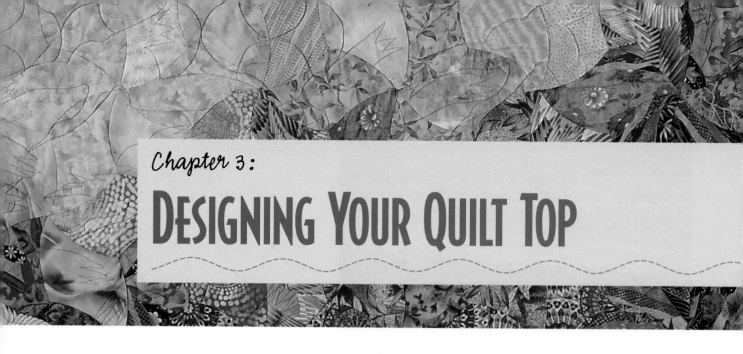

Chapter 3:
DESIGNING YOUR QUILT TOP

Your one-patch quilt top will be constructed mostly of one simple shape; of course, you'll need a template to make sure all the pieces you cut are of uniform size.

In this chapter, we'll show you how to draft your own quilt top. If you prefer, you can purchase a commercial template from one of the many companies listed in the Resources section at the end of this book.

CHOOSING THE RIGHT COMMERCIAL TEMPLATE

Basically, three types of commercial templates exist: solid acrylic, slotted acrylic, and the metal "outline" type, which has the center cut out a quarter inch from the edge and is backed with a non-skid, sandpaper-like material.

All three types let you see through to the material below, allowing you to "fussy cut" your fabrics with ease. So, which type should you choose?

If you are a hand-piecer, you may want to pick either the slotted acrylic or metal templates. The slotted acrylic type has a row of "windows" a quarter inch from the edge, so you can mark guidelines for the seam lines, as well as for the cutting lines. And the metal templates, which are exactly a quarter-inch wide, are also designed to let you mark both seam and cutting lines.

If you will be using a rotary cutter, choose either the solid or slotted acrylic templates both of which have plenty of room for your fingers to hold them down without getting in the way of the blade.

The metal templates, having such a narrow surface, really aren't safe with rotary cutters. No matter how careful you are, it's all too easy for a fingertip to stray over the edge into harm's way. And while it's OK to put "sweat and tears" into your art, it's best to keep the blood to a minimum. One additional note on rotary cutting: If you haven't yet tried the new, smaller rotary cutters with dime-sized blades, you might want to do so with your next project. I find that they work especially well with the curved templates because of the exceptional maneuverability they offer. Keep in mind, that these mini-cutters will only go through one layer of fabric. One drawback is that the blades dull easier and faster. For cutting many layers of fabric, I prefer the small 28 millimeter cutter.

My personal preference when cutting my pieces is to use a rotary cutter, placing my acrylic template on the right side of the fabric. That way, I can really see all the details when I want to "fussy cut." As you will soon learn, that it is a method I use often.

And to make sure my pieces and yours come out exactly the way we want them to, I've designed my own line of templates with two handy features:

☐ First there is a center line marked on top of each template to help you lay it on a seam when strip piecing is desired.

☐ Second, seam lines are indicated with a dotted line a quarter inch from the edge of the template. So, by placing it on your fabric and looking at the area between the dotted lines, you can see exactly what will be visible once the piece is sewn.

MAKING YOUR OWN TEMPLATES

It's easy to make a template that's a simple geometric shape like a square, rectangle, or equilateral triangle. Just take a sheet of template plastic with graph lines on it and draw the shape you desire.

But what if you want a more complicated shape? What if you can't find a commercial source for it, or you simply can't wait to get started? Fortunately, it's not at all difficult. Let's look at a few examples…

Drafting a Kite Template:

Take a look at the **Northern Exposure** quilt on page 12. This attractive piece was constructed entirely out of kite-shaped pieces of fabric. And making your own kite template takes only a few minutes.

Start by drafting an equilateral triangle where each side is 7 ¾ inches. Then, draw a line perpendicular to the center on each side of the triangle, and stop when the lines intersect. You now have three identical shapes each of which is a kite. See page 65 for Kite template pattern.

Drafting a Curved Kite Template:

Now, look at the quilt **Sandhill Cranes of Nebraska** on page 5. It's made with a curved kite template, which is a slight variation of the kite pattern.

To create a curved kite template, take the kite template you've already made; erase one side at a time; and then curve it either outward or inward, using the "Rob Peter To Pay Paul" method. See page 66 for Curved Kite template pattern.

Drafting a Half Hexagon Template:

The wonderful quilt **Country Sunset** by Carol Wight Jones on page 18 is made using the half hexagon shape.

Country Sunset (half hexagon) 48" x 57"
Carol Wight Jones, Anchorage, Alaska 1997

To make a half hexagon template, draft another equilateral triangle 7 ¾ inches on each side. Then, divide each side into three equal sections.

Now, find the spot that is one-third of the way along each side, draw a line that is parallel to the closest side, and stop where these lines intersect. You now have a triangle containing three half hexagons and can use any of them as a template. See page 67 for Half Hexagon template pattern.

Drafting a 30°-30°-120° Isosceles Triangle Template.

We aren't finished yet. We have even more tricks up our sleeves to create even more wonderful one patches, like the quilt *Laconia Sunset* by Cathy Andrew of Westwood, MA on page 15.

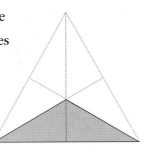

Once more, start by drafting a 7 ¾-inch equilateral triangle. Now find its center by drawing a light line perpendicular to the center of each side. (The center is where these lines intersect.)

Put the point of your pencil at the center of the triangle, and draw a heavier line to each of its corners. You now have three 30°-30°-120° isosceles triangles. (The degree numbers refer to the size of the angles at the corners.) See page 68 for Isosceles Triangle template pattern.

Drafting a Curved Diamond Template.

Our next template shape, the curved diamond, is one of my favorites. An example, *Xian Hé,* by Vicki Carlson, is shown on page 47.

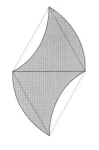

I introduced this shape in 1994 in an article in The International Quilter, which showed how to create one-of-a-kind quilts using curved shapes with a little twist. I'll be telling you more about that twist in a later chapter.

The curved diamond template is actually a variation on a regular diamond. To create it, draft two equilateral triangles with one side touching to form a diamond shape.

Then, use the same "Rob Peter To Pay Paul" procedure you did to create your curved kite template, taking a curved piece off of one side and adding it to the opposite side. Voila! The curved diamond is born. See page 69 for Curved Diamond template pattern.

Drafting a Half Clamshell Template.

A favorite of many of my students is the half clamshell.

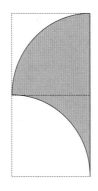

To draft it, draw two three-inch squares side by side. Once this is done, use a compass to create the two curves needed to draw the half clamshell. See page 70 for Half Clamshell template pattern.

Drafting the Flowing Ribbon Template.

To draft the flowing ribbon template, draw three three-inch squares as illustrated here. Once this is done, use a compass to create the two curves needed to create the

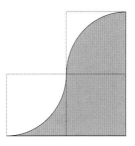

flowing ribbon. See page 71 for Flowing Ribbon template pattern.

September Coneflowers 40" x 44"
Ann Fahl, Racine, Wisconsin 2005

Other One-Patch Designs

Amazing, isn't it? In one short chapter, you've learned to create seven different one-patch templates. There are many more to choose from, including the most basic; the square. Simple squares can be used to create absolutely fantastic works of art. Watercolor quilts are abundant proof.

Take a look at the magnificent quilt on this page, where well-known quilter Ann Fahl* uses squares embellished with her now-famous cone-flowers. As another example my **Blue Lagoon** quilt on page 21 which uses simple nine-patches that give you a chance to experiment with a huge variety of colors and textures. Hopefully, these pictures will whet your appetite for our further discussion on the nine-patch, included in the upcoming chapter on sewing your quilt.

Blue Lagoon 40" x 40"
Louisa L. Smith, Loveland, Colorado 1995

By now, you've probably selected the shape you want to use to create your one-patch quilt. (If not, you may want to read Chapter 3 to help you decide.)

Before you start cutting your fabric, I'd like to share a few tips that can make this part of the process a lot more creative—and more fun!

First, I recommend cutting at least three shapes from each fabric—provided, of course, that you have enough fabric to do so. I have found this an easy way to get started. You can eliminate or add to that amount as needed. That way, you'll have enough of each fabric to make your design flow smoothly.

Second, if you're going to be using a rotary cutter, it's a very good idea to purchase a turntable, which will make your cutting much easier and faster, especially with curved shapes.

If you don't want to buy a turntable (see Resources pages 76-77), you can achieve much the same result by putting your cutting mat on the corner of a table where you are able to move yourself from side-to-side as you are cutting. A small cutting board (the kind with a shiny bottom to make it turn easily) also works well, provided your pieces are smaller than a half-yard so you can manipulate them easily.

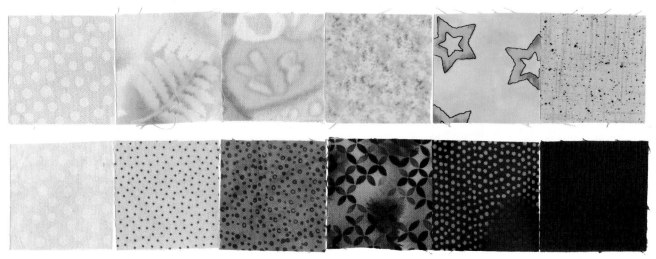

Figure 1. Color transitions.

I like to work with gradations. For instance, if I'm working with red, I don't just buy one red fabric, but lots of different shades and textures. It's also highly desirable to include reds that incorporate other colors, like yellow and orange as well. This not only makes your quilt sparkle; it also makes it much easier to connect your red to other color families. Take a look at Figure 1 showing the sample of color transitions, because seeing, is believing!

To get a better understanding of how to create a bridge from one color family to the next, look at the fabric swatches. See how each different yellow we have chosen blends into the next. Then see how you can gradually switch to a green section, on the one hand, or orange, on the other. The transition pieces are usually fabrics that include two or more colors. But there is also another way to gradually change from one color to another.

To see how, take a moment to study the quilt *Java Revisited* on page 37. In this piece, I wanted to create a focal point with a fuchsia-colored flower. However, I didn't want a bull's-eye effect that would jar the eye and seem disconnected from the rest of the quilt.

To accomplish my goal, I introduced the fuchsia in a small way near the flower by strip-piecing two fabrics and then cutting a Curved Diamond shape out of

Aloha From Kauai (half clamshell) 44 ½" x 47"
Judith Sabourin, Medfield, MA 2007

them. I also used a green fabric that had some fuchsia in it. This resulted in a much more pleasing composition. Why? I believe it's because the eye sometimes needs a bit of repetition to accustom itself to a major transition.

This little trick of strip-piecing fabrics and then cutting shapes out of them gives you an additional tool to make your transitions.

To create strips of the proper width, measure your template from the center to one edge, and add ½-inch (¼-inch for each side) for the seam allowance. Piece two of these strips together. Then use your template to cut the shape you will use in your quilt. (See curved kite piecing on page 30.) If you're using my line of acrylic templates, this is simple to do because they have the center lines already marked on them.
All you have to do is place that line directly over the seam and rotary-cut your shape. Another tip is that

sometimes you may want the seam line to be off-center. See Figure 2 where the samples of black 'n white can create motion in your piece. Simply mark your template with a permanent marker for easy placement.

Another useful tip is to fussy-cut shapes to create a repetition of design, or to follow the lines of design on the fabric. This is a great technique for creating a sense of motion. (See Figure 2 where I placed my templates to make the pattern appear as if it is spinning, to enhance the overall composition.)

To make it easier to get precisely the look you have in mind, simply take a permanent marker and trace the design you want to fussy cut onto your acrylic template. A little rubbing alcohol will remove the markings after you're done, leaving your templates looking like new!

While you're cutting shapes, you should also be placing them on your design wall. Placing your shapes is the most time-consuming step of the project, but it's also the most important. So, be patient and play with them.

One method we used was to create a grid of the shapes on the computer using the template we wanted, in this case the Kite shape. (Template grids can be found on pages 72-75.) We then copied the grid onto on transparency film and laid it

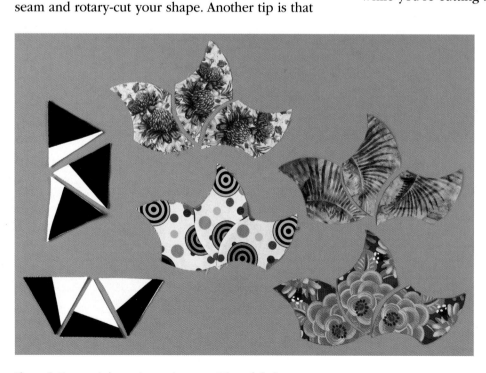

Figure 2. Fussy cut shapes to create a repetition of design.

on top of the design. This aided in choosing the fabric colors, giving us something to follow when laying out the pieces on the fabric wall.

Another way to create your composition I used in my quilt, **Northern Exposure** (page 12). I arranged all of my fabrics on a table, ranging from lightest to darkest. I then cut six kite shapes from each fabric, except the first and last. Only three were needed from them. I constructed three pieces from fabric #1 with three pieces from fabric #2 into hexagonal shapes. Next, I took the other three pieces from fabric #2, and three pieces from fabric #3, and constructed another hexagonal shape. I kept making hexagonal shapes and I was able to do this while traveling, since I didn't need a design wall at this point. Only after completion of all my hexagonal shapes did I start placing them on the design wall. And yes, some of them did not make it into the quilt! The composition worked out very well for me.

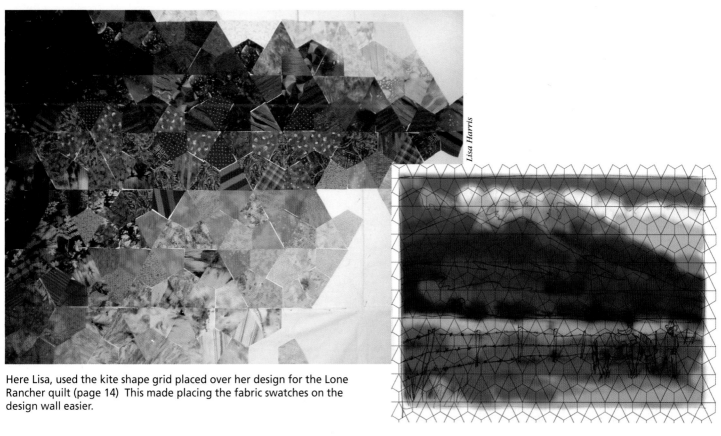

Lisa Harris

Here Lisa, used the kite shape grid placed over her design for the Lone Rancher quilt (page 14) This made placing the fabric swatches on the design wall easier.

On this quilt the light source is in the center and gradually moves darker towards the outside edges.

On Golden Pond (half clamshell) 41″ x 57″
Cookie Warner, Fort Collins, CO 2003

Choose one point as the light source and make all your colors graduate out from it. Your light source can be anywhere in your composition. But wherever it is, it's where you should put your lightest colored pieces. Then, gradually move out in all directions, getting a little bit darker as you go. To see how effective includ-

ing a light source can be, look at **Northern Exposure** on page 12 (where the light source is located in the bottom right-hand corner), and **Java Revisited** on page 37 (where it's in the upper left-hand corner).

Where should you put the light source in your quilt? Here are some placement ideas to help you decide.

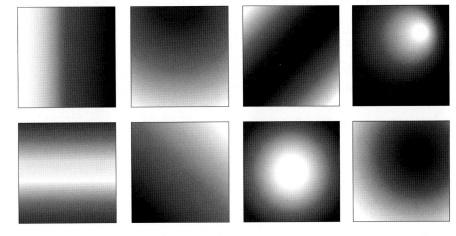

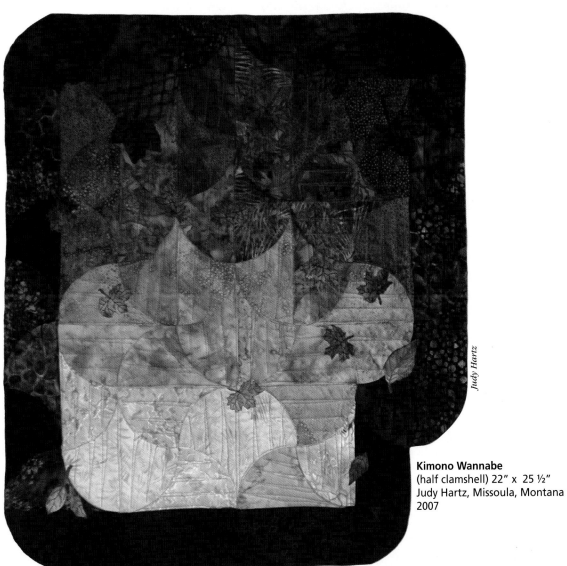

Judy Hartz

Kimono Wannabe
(half clamshell) 22" x 25 ½"
Judy Hartz, Missoula, Montana
2007

Note how the light source on this quilt is at the bottom and gradually becomes darker toward the top.

Chapter 5

SEWING YOUR QUILT

Let's take another look at your shapes, but this time we'll explore piecing procedures.

NEW WAYS WITH SQUARES

We'll start with the simplest of shapes; the square. For inspiration, turn for a moment to *September Coneflowers* on page 20, a quilt by Ann Fahl* of Racine, Wisconsin, that provides a great example of a background composed entirely of squares. Ann always keeps stacks of six-inch squares on hand and uses them to create her patchwork backgrounds. Then she does her famous free-motion embroidery, as explained in her must-read book, Coloring with Thread.*

I won't waste your time rehashing the use of squares for the watercolor technique, as there are many good books on the subject. But I would like to discuss using small nine-patches to create the base for your quilt top.

I find that a good size for such squares is one inch. So, start by cutting strips from your collected fabrics that are 1-½ inches wide.

As you know, in a traditional nine-patch, you generally work with contrasting fabrics (five dark and four light, or five light and four dark). And each nine-patch block is made up of three rows, in this case, three 1-½" squares (including seam allowance).

This contrast between dark and light is what makes the nine-patch design work, but I use a lot less contrast in my nine-patches then you would normally. We're still going to play with this contrast. But this time, instead of using just two fabrics, we may use as many as nine!

Considering how much easier the nine patch is to construct with strip-piecing methods, it should come as no surprise that it's how we're going to construct ours.

First, we'll piece together three different strips of fabric to make our units. (We'll call these three-strip combinations our strata, or sets.) To get as many different combinations as possible, you'll need to cut each of your 1-½ inch strips into thirds—so instead of measuring 45" long, they'll be only about 14 inches long.

The strata are sewn with either a light/dark/light combination or a dark/light/dark combination. Then, you'll cut these combinations into 1-½ inch sections to construct your nine-patches.

* See Resources.

Before you start, I have one more trick up my sleeve that I'd like to share. Before I start sewing strata, I arrange all of my strips in order—from very lightest to the very darkest—on my work surface. This makes it so much fun to pick fabrics for each strata. It also reminds you to have some contrast, though not at much contrast as with a regular nine-patch.

Construct nine-patches that range from very light to very dark. (Take a look at figure 3 below for examples.) Then, only after you have completed this step, place them on your design wall and play with the arrangement of the nine-patch blocks.

It's so much fun, I guarantee you will be hooked if you try it just once! So now that you know how it works, take another look at the *Blue Lagoon* quilt on page 21 to see how effective it can be.

KITES AND CURVED KITES THAT LET YOUR IMAGINATION SOAR

Now, let's proceed to the Kite shape. Basically, it offers you two choices: You can either sew your kites into equilateral triangles or into hexagons. See figure 4. (I used hexagons for the *Northern Exposure* quilt on page 12, but Lisa used the equilateral triangle method in her quilt *Lone Rancher* quilt page 14.)

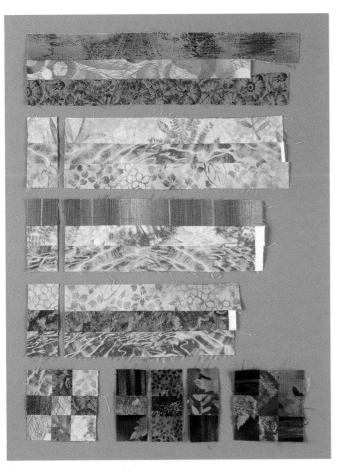

Figure 3. Nine patch piecing procedure.

Figure 4. Kite piecing procedure.

Both procedures are quite simple. Just create rows, and then sew them together to produce similar results and complete your quilt top. (Take a moment now to look at figure 4 kite piecing procedures.)

Now before we go onto the curved shapes, we will follow one simple rule. Always begin sewing the seam ¼-inch in and finish sewing the seam ¼-inch from the edge. This will make the pieces fit into one another perfectly and will make the pressing so easy! Make sure you look at figure 5 the procedure for pressing your pieces.

The Curved Kites follow the same procedures as the Kites. When pinning the edges of the Curved Kite together, be sure to position the rounded, convex part (I think of it as the "belly") on the bottom, and the indented, concave part (I call it the "bite") on the top. This puts the fuller part of the seam allowance up where you can manipulate it easily, so you don't wind up with little pleats in the seam. This rule applies to all the curved seams in this book. Placing the edges

Figure 6. Curved Kite piecing procedure.

even and finding the middle or half way point is crucial. You can always find the halfway point of a curved seam by folding the piece in half and creasing it. Follow these steps and your curved seams are a snap (see figure 5):

1. Bellies are ALWAYS on the bottom,
2. Always leave the ¼-inch at the beginning and end of the seams open; and
3. Don't forget to pin at the halfway mark.

Figure 5. Procedure for pressing the pieces.

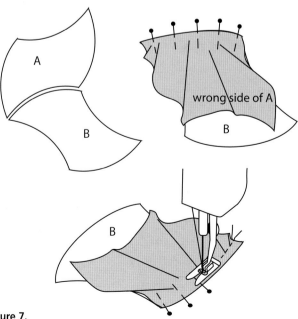

Figure 7.

I always use plenty of pins and position them carefully, so I have absolutely no difficulty sewing these shapes. If you find you have difficulty, there is a tool called the Curved Master Pressure Foot* that seems to be a good alternative for some quilters. As with any tool, you have to learn how to use it, it then becomes quite second nature and can be very helpful in constructing the small curved shapes.

TRIANGLES, HALF HEXAGONS, AND CURVED DIAMONDS

Piecing equilateral triangles poses no problem because they have straight edges.

The same procedure also works for Half-Hexagons (or Trapezoids) and Isosceles Triangles. Just lay them out in the shape of an equilateral triangle. See figure 8. Then sew the equilateral triangles you've constructed into rows to complete your quilt top.

* See Resources.

As for Curved Diamonds, there really is only one easy method; sew them in sets of three, thus creating hexagonal shapes. See figure 9 piecing diagram. Then, sew these hexagons into rows and join the rows. Combining smaller units into larger ones always seems to make the construction process easier!

Remember too, when you're playing with Curved Diamonds, you can use them to create flower-like shapes.

Remember back in Quilting 101, when you learned how to piece six diamond shapes into a six-pointed star? Well, the curved diamond works the same way! (Take a look at *Java Revisited* on page 37, and you'll see what I mean.)

However, it would be quite a task to sew these flower-like shapes to each other. It is therefore important that you construct the curved diamonds in sets of three only.

Figure 8. Equilateral triangle, isosceles triangle and half hexagon piecing procedures.

Figure 9. Curved Diamond piecing procedure.

HALF CLAMSHELL AND MUCH MORE

The Half-Clamshell is very versatile because it is one of the few templates you can cut regular and reversed. There are two ways to approach this wonderful shape: A very simple method or a more complicated method.

Let us first explore the simpler method. You can actually cut shapes both regular, and you can turn the template and cut them reversed. The trick is to place the pieces on the design wall, making sure you will always put four pieces in a block formation, thus creating a six-inch block. Four regular pieces make a block, and four reversed pieces can make a block. When you place a regular block adjacent to a reverse block you can create a full-clamshell. When you put a regular block next to a regular block, you create an apple-core

design. (See figure 10 piecing procedure of the easy method.) Look at the quilt **Wind Dancer** on page 50 by Joan Rossi. It was constructed in the easy method.

Figure 10. Easy Clamshell piecing procedure.

Now, for the more complicated method, and one I really enjoy very much. You can cut shapes regular and reverse, just as before. But, when placing them on the design wall, you will not pay any attention to creating blocks. In fact, you will soon realize you can place them in such a way that they create, what I refer to as, 1-½ blocks. With this method you can add "odd" shapes. These odd shapes can be a half-circle, a full circle and yes, other interesting shapes, all parts of the Half Clamshell template. You can even cross-cut some

Figure 11. Advanced Clamshell piecing procedure.

shapes to make the shapes fit into one another. (See Figure 11 piecing procedure.)

Believe me, this is not hard. I'm always looking for the simplest construction methods. All you have to do to use this method is arrange the pieces on your design wall, and then sew!

The arranging part is absolutely critical. Be sure to allow yourself plenty of time to try different combinations. I refer to this part of the process as "playing," because I indeed play a lot and this step may take days. It is crucial to continually rearrange the pieces. Once you are completely satisfied with your composition, you can start to piece the shapes. Taking digital images is helpful because you can see instantly where the composition is not working or refer back to previous compositions.

A great tip for moving pieces from your design wall to your sewing machine or favorite armchair is to pin a small section to a paper towel. This keeps everything in the correct order and even lets you transport your project to soccer practice or the doctor's waiting room if you are hand-piecing.

You can also mark the paper towels with numbers, so you'll always put the sewn pieces back in the right place. On teaching trips, I usually travel with an assortment of pieces pinned to several different paper towels, all numbered to keep them organized. When I return home, I simply pin them back on my design wall, which I've marked with corresponding numbers. This saves a great deal of time and frustration and makes sure the composition you've spent so much time on turns out just right!

HAND-PIECING TIPS

I really do a lot of hand-piecing, and because I travel a lot, I always have some on hand. Spending many hours in airports and on planes, I have learned to hand-piece fast and enjoy it. Below are some tips for you. You already know how I pin shapes from my design wall to a paper towel.

What you will need is a sharp and thin needle, such as a Milliners #10 or #11 (also used for hand appliqué). They will glide through the fabric easily and are long enough to hold a lot of small stitches at one time. Using good cotton thread is helpful as well; it does not knot or fray so easily. I take small stitches, as many as I can get on my needle, and I use my left hand to put those on the needle by flipping it back and forth. My right hand only holds the needle in place. (See figure 12 hand piecing procedure.)

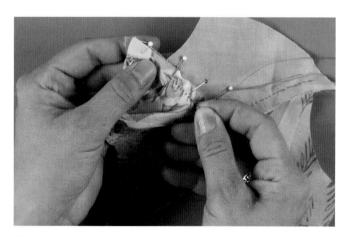

Figure 12.

Try it: I have a feeling you will love it as well. Do I use both machine and hand-piecing in one quilt? You bet I do! My small machine stitches match up with my small hand stitches just fine. As soon as I am home from a trip, I definitely use my sewing machine.

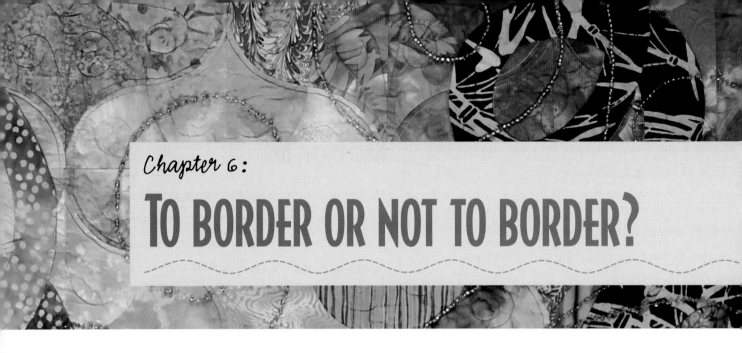

Chapter 6:
TO BORDER OR NOT TO BORDER?

After you've sewn all of your shapes together to form your quilt top, it's time to step back, take a good hard look, and ask yourself, "Do I need a border or not?"

You'll want to consider this question carefully, because sometimes a piece is just fine as is, and all you need to do is bind the edges. Other times, you'll want to add one or more borders to make your finished quilt or wall hanging the size you desire. Still other times, you'll realize your top is virtually crying out for you to add another design element.

If your piece does need a border, I'd strongly suggest you start by reviewing all the quilts in this book, because they offer some great ideas to get your creative juices flowing.

Perhaps the top you've constructed has curved edges, or edges that are irregular in some other way. If so, the first step is to decide how to deal with them.

To even them out, you can simply cut the irregular edges, bind them, or add a straight border. Simply lay your top on your cutting mat and trim the edges, making sure you use a large cutting board. Remember to use the lines on your mat to keep your piece straight, so the

square or rectangle you wind up with will be even. If you have cut the edge off you may need another step, the stay-stitching step. Because the edges now are really bias edges and can stretch, you need to stitch about $^1/_8$-inch from the edge of your quilt top with a large stitch (4.0). Do this on all four sides. Lay your quilt top flat on a table or on the floor, and pull up on some of the stitches here and there, gathering them, to shrink the outer edge and keep your quilt top square. This will ensure all sides will be even. If you are happy and they indeed measure the same, just take an iron and press where you pulled the stitches up. A little bit of spray starch works wonders as well. This procedure should be followed before binding or borders are added.

Another option with a curved-edge composition is to turn the curves into a major design element by letting them weave in and out of your border.

To see how these techniques work, take a look at the quilt *Xian Hé* on page 47, where the maker has left some edges curved and cut others straight. Note especially how the dark border touches the quilt where it is predominantly light and the light border touches the quilt where it is predominantly dark. This method is called: negative/positive.

In **Sandhill Cranes of Nebraska** on page 5, I wanted pieced borders that reflected the quilt's colors and kept the light source intact.

I also wanted borders with mitered corners (ones that are joined on the diagonal like a picture frame, and I wanted the design of the borders to appear to flow into the quilt in places. So, I developed the following method.

The Framed Borders Method

Measure each side of your quilt top. Now, if the quilt is even (meaning the edges are even) this is not a problem. But if your quilt has irregular curves, such as the curved diamond shapes, you must measure where the curve comes into the quilt the most; that is the shortest measurement. See figure 13. In this method, we are sewing the borders to each other with mitered corners *prior to* adding them to the quilt top. In fact, you are actually constructing a picture frame with your borders and then adding them to your quilt top.

It will be much easier if you refer to the pictures in Project #4, Curved Diamond on pages 60-63, where we have used this method to add borders to the quilt. This Framed Borders method works just as well if you have uneven borders, meaning your border is much wider on one side than on the other. You lay the framed border on your table or floor and center your quilt top on it. Now you can "experiment"! For example where do I want part of the quilt design to come into my border, and where do I want to add just the border? In Java Revisited, I simply laid the quilt top on the frame and hand appliquéed it on. This means the quilt is really

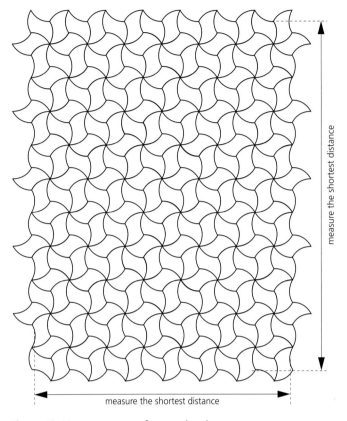

measure the shortest distance

measure the shortest distance

Figure 13. How to measure for your borders.

lying on top of the border. You can audition a wide variety of positions before sewing.

If you have miscalculated, and in some places there is a space between the quilt top and the framed border; fear not, because you can always add more shapes to the edges of your quilt top!

To see how this framed border method works, look closely at the edges of **Sandhill Cranes of Nebraska,** page 5. Notice where two hexagonal shapes are placed onto the left border, while the bottom left border has three shapes. If you'd like to see other examples of the framed border method, check out **Java Revisited** on page 37, **Xian Hé** on page 47, and **Butterflies are Free** on page 48.

THE NEGATIVE/POSITIVE BORDER

In *Java Revisited*, where I also used the framed border method, I created what I call the Negative/Positive Border as part of my picture frame.

This distinctive effect is a great way to add a sense of movement to your quilt, and it's a lot easier to create than it looks. Here's the procedure in a nutshell:

Measure all sides of your quilt top. No need to use math to create this incredibly effective border. You just need the length and width of your quilt top. Because the edges are uneven and some come way inside the quilt, you will need to measure from the most inward point. My quilt top measured 39 ½ inches by 52 inches. (See figure 14.)

I want to create a frame of my borders so that I can place the quilt on it. I decided to have my borders be

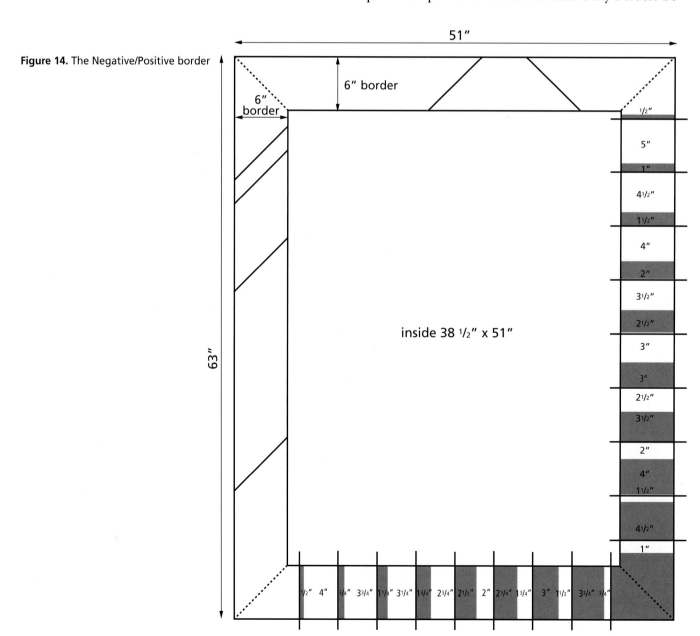

Figure 14. The Negative/Positive border

Java Revisted (curved diamond) 51" x 63"
Louisa L. Smith, Loveland, Colorado 1994

six inches wide, which is an ideal measurement for the irregular curved diamond shape edges.

When you have a frame, you have two measurements; the inside and the outside. I start with the inside measurement which was 39 ½ inches by 52 inches, I make it a little smaller to make sure I have all the inward curves covered my measurements will have to be: 38 ½ inches by 51 inches.

The outside of my frame will be: 38 ½" + 12" (6 " of border for each side) = 50 ½ " by 51" + 12" (6 " of border for each side) = 63".

Having the measurements of the frame is all you need to begin. Cut your dark (positive) and light (negative) fabric of your choice into 6 ½" strips. I always start by cutting two of each, and you can always cut others if needed. I want to make blocks in my borders that will enable me to gradually change from dark fabric to light fabric.

A lot of math is not necessary, and you can fudge a lot because it is the visual you are after. I took 9 blocks of 5 ½ inches for my long side and just used the Rob Peter To Pay Paul method to create the blocks. That simply means take from the dark and give to the light side. (See figure 14.) You will notice in each block the dark fabric gets bigger as the light fabric gets smaller, or the other way around.

The shorter, or bottom border was constructed the same way, except I opted for 8 blocks which measured 4 ½ inches wide. See? No difficult math involved here.

So, let me recap: The long side was to have 9 blocks and the short side, 8 blocks.

Are you with me so far? The math is simply this: $9 \times 5\frac{1}{2} = 49\frac{1}{2}$; but my outside measurement is 63". Subtracting 49 ½ from 63 = 13 ½. . So I just add 6-½ inches of dark border fabric to the dark end and 7 inches of light border fabric on the light end and make it all come out to 63 inches. That is how easy it is; you can make the last and first blocks of the border any size you want. Just make sure they are the right colors.

Despite varying sized blocks on the side and bottom borders, they won't appear noticeably different, and won't change the wonderful look you've created. It is the visual impact of the Negative/Positive border that you are after.

A FINAL WORD ON BORDERS

For another example of the dark-against-light and light-against-dark technique, see Blue Lagoon on page 21. No borders were attached here, but the lights and darks of the nine patches were placed to give the illusion of a border.

In this case, the *shapes themselves add a border,* (see the ***Hawaiian Quilt*** on page 39 ***Kimono Wannabe*** quilt on page 27). Here too, the shapes created a border instantly. Are these not great examples of easy and creative borders? Before we leave the subject of borders, be sure to check out Carol Wight Jones' ***Country Sunset*** on page 18

Kimono Inspired (mixed patterns) 49" x 51"
Louisa Smith, Loveland, CO 2008

Fall Fest (half clamshell) 42" x 51"
Dwyta Schroeder, Honolulu, HI 2007

as another example of using the shapes as the border. The inner border of pink is about one inch wide, while the outer border repeats the same half-hexagons of which the top is composed, giving the quilt a unified look.

Carol also uses small piping instead of conventional binding; a technique for which she is famous. As you can see, the combination works beautifully and gives you one more source of inspiration to draw on in creating your own masterpieces!

Chapter 7

ADDING EMBELLISHMENTS

Now we come to my favorite part of the creative process embellishment, and it may soon become your favorite part too. Not only does it let you hide mistakes and camouflage places where your composition isn't working as well as you'd like; but it also adds sparkle and pizzazz to your completed project.

I want every one of my quilts to be the very best it can be. So after I've completed my top, it goes right back on my design wall. If there are spots that are jarring to the eye, or areas that could use a little extra energy, I cover them up with a carefully considered piece of appliqué.

Sometimes, I'm quite happy with my composition, but feel I'm not telling the quilt's "story" as well as I could be. Here, too, embellishment is the answer.

ADDING SHIMMER WITH BEADING

Take **Northern Exposure** on page 12, for instance. The snowflakes were an obvious choice to convey the feeling of cold winter days. But snow isn't a flat white. It glistens in the sun. So, while I was hand quilting, I added a bead every few stitches. Because this bead-n-quilt technique was one easy step, I was able to add a special touch without putting in hours of extra effort.

As for the snowflakes, they are made from Ultra-suede, and they were beaded into place. Which means I eliminated a step by not having to sew the image on first and then bead it, but rather, bead and sew, all at once.

EXPERIMENTING WITH FREEZER PAPER SHAPES

Sandhill Cranes of Nebraska is another example of a quilt where getting the embellishment just right was absolutely critical. See the detail view of the paper shapes on page 41.

This piece was inspired by the incredible sight my husband and I came upon while driving to a teaching engagement in Nebraska. As we rounded a bend in the road at sunset, we came upon a gathering of not just thousands, but tens of thousands, of these magnificent birds. We pulled to the side of the road, and I grabbed my camera.

Obviously, the resulting quilt would feature the cranes against a sunset background. But how many cranes

Detail of freezer paper shapes on the quilt **Sandhill Cranes of Nebraska.**

appliqué or fabric painting, but when I went back to my photos, I realized that black silhouettes were that was truly visible in my photograph.

After briefly thinking about using specialty fabrics, I settled on freezer paper cut-outs to adhere to plain black cotton fabric, and affixed them to the top with needleturn appliqué.

Happily, this solution was both easier and more effective than the other options I had considered.

MORE APPLIQUÉ OPTIONS

Summer Bouquet on page 61 is another excellent example of using hand appliqué to enhance the theme of a quilt. Plus adding images to your quilt can be fun and easy, thanks to the many products available at your local quilt shop or fabric store.

I love working with both Wonder-Under* and Steam-A-Seam II*. The latter is especially good for helping you decide where to position your appliqués because it has a tacky surface that lets you stick them on your quilt, then remove them and try them somewhere else.

Thus, you can "audition" your pieces over and over stepping back to give each arrangement a critical evaluation until you find the one that's just right. No pinning or basting is ever necessary!

should there be? What size and color should I make them? Where should I position them for maximum effect?

To decide, I cut a huge variety of crane templates, ranging from 3 to 10 inches, out of brown paper and began playing with them.

Originally, I intended to have them "migrating" all over the quilt and graduating in size, but somehow, no matter how I positioned them, none of the arrangements I came up with seemed satisfying.

It was only when I took some of the templates to my local copying store and blew them up to about 21 inches that this quilt began to come together. I experimented with making the birds their natural color with

* See Resources.

ATTACHING YOUR APPLIQUÉS

Once all your appliqué pieces are positioned to your satisfaction, you can iron them in place. Then, you have several options for finishing the edges.

Detail of **Fall Splendor** (curved diamond) 37" x 36" Susan Gerhardt, South Thomaston, ME 2004

You can machine-appliqué your edges with a satin stitch or buttonhole stitch. Or, you can thread-paint them with a technique that is sometimes called free-motion embroidery.

For a closer look at thread-painting, see the **On Golden Pond** quilt on page 26, which also uses this technique.

I usually use the satin stitch in my quilts, partly because it helps them stand up to all the handling they get in my classes and lectures, and I prefer Sulky® thread, because it comes in such a broad array of

Detail of thread painting on the quilt **On Golden Pond.**

colors. If your quilts won't be subjected to too much wear and tear, you may just opt for Steam-A-Seam II, combined with a bit of machine quilting to hold your edges in place.

CREATING 3-D EFFECTS

Want to add a three-dimensional effect to your quilt? Try lined appliqué, the technique used on my **Blue Lagoon** quilt on page 21.

The procedure for making fish (or any other creature or object you choose) "come alive" against your background is as follows:

1. Cut your object out of printed fabric, leaving a quarter-inch seam allowance all around.

2. Turn the wrong side of your printed fabric toward you, and lay it on top of a piece of black fabric.

3. Sew around the image you wish to make 3-D with tiny stitches. (Use the 1.5 stitch setting on your sewing machine.)

To create this marvelous embellishment, she sewed two shapes together and then turned them inside out, as if she were making a tiny quilt. Then she attached this to an identical shape in her pieced top, and voila! A butterfly was born! And it flutters magically over life-like leaves, created using the same ingenious method.

4. Trim your seam allowance as close as possible to your stitches, but not so close that they're in danger of coming out. ($1/16$" or so should be about right.)

5. Cut a small slit in the center of the black fabric. (Take care not to cut through the printed layer.) Make the slit just large enough to be able to turn the piece inside out.

6. After turning inside out, iron the piece, and quilt it, if desired.

7. Tack the black lining of your appliqué to your quilt top by hand, in such a way as to hide the slit. Leave the edges of the appliqué loose to create the 3-D effect you're aiming for.

8. Add other embellishments, if desired. (In Blue Lagoon, I sewed on pearl-colored beads in graduated sizes to simulate bubbles coming up from the fish.)

For another wonderful example of 3-D appliqués, take a look at the flowers and leaves gracing Josephine McCoy's *Forest Floor* on page 44. Notice, too, the clever way she added a butterfly, using extra curved diamond shapes.

In *Country Sunset* on page 18, Carol Wight Jones employed some additional 3-D techniques. She sliced a two-inch wide strip of dark green Ultrasuede* at about $1/8$" to $1/4$" intervals, leaving about $1/4$" uncut. Then, she manipulated several of these strips to form pine needle clusters and added ruched pinecones made from brown fabric, a method developed by Anita Shackelford*.

* See Resources.

Ultra Suede,® a wonderful fabric that needn't be turned under because since it won't ravel, was also used in Northern Exposure on page 12 to create the appliquéed and beaded snowflakes.

I have yet another method I call: Free-Form Appliqué. For an example, take a look at the detail from **Blue Lagoon** quilt here. The seaweed on the lower right hand side of the quilt is free-form appliquéed. It is quite difficult to attach something as lacy as seaweed and hand appliqué it. As this would be an incredible chore, here is my solution: Cut the image out of your fabric with small sharp scissors. The image is so small in most areas it is virtually impossible to appliqué or even adhere to the quilt. Take a Styrofoam™ meat tray, place the cut image on it right side down and wet the entire image with FrayCheck.® Let it dry, peel it off, and place on the quilt where desired. You can bead it on or you can sew it on by using embroidery thread right through the middle of the seaweed. I used a metallic thread in mine and added beading to the piece. In other words, it will not fray so put it on any way you desire. Take another look at the close-up, it is fantastic. If use or handling starts to make the appliqués look

Detail of seaweed appliqué on the quilt **Blue Lagoon.**

Forest Floor (curved diamond) 72" x 49"
Josephine McCoy, Fort Collins, CO 2000

bad, simply iron the quilt and it will look as good as new. Try this technique—it is so much fun.

FURTHER ADVENTURES IN EMBELLISHMENT

Embellishment techniques are truly limited only to your imagination, and you can use just about anything your heart desires.

For example, you can use fabric paints to fix a spot on you quilt where you are unhappy with the color. You can also add hand or machine embroidery. My Janome MC11000 sewing machine has the capability to add just about anything I like. With it, I can copy parts of the fabric in embroidery so that I can reproduce the elements on other parts of my quilt. How cool is that? The quilt *Obsession 2,* below, uses both fabric paints and machine embroidery as embellishment.

Why not consider putting one or more of them to work in your next quilt? For added inspiration, pick up a copy of ***Exploring Textile Arts*** and **Contemporary Quilts, Design, Surface and Stitch,**** two books I highly recommend.

Then just envision your quilt top as a canvas and let your imagination go wild!

Obsession 2 (half clamshell) 52" x 49"
Louisa Smith, Loveland, CO 2007

* See Resources.

Chapter 8

QUILTING YOUR TOP

Now that your quilt top is finished, the next step is to quilt the three layers together. But before you pick up your needle, take a moment to think about your quilt backing.

TIPS ON BACKING YOUR QUILT

This is the perfect place to use all those shapes you cut but didn't use. You can piece them together to create a section of your backing. Or if you have only a few pieces left, you can use them to create a label, which you'll then appliqué onto the backing before sandwiching your quilt. (After appliquéing your label, make sure to cut away the backing fabric behind it to eliminate extra bulk that would make quilting more difficult.)

A pieced backing is a terrific solution when you don't have yardage that's quite big enough by itself. One great way to piece your backing is to add a diagonal strip across it.

This is a very economical method, ideal for wall hangings and baby quilts that are just a teensy bit over 44 inches wide, because it makes your fabric "grow" both horizontally and vertically.

Simply fold your square or rectangular backing on the diagonal, and cut it on the crease. This will leave you with two triangular pieces that have bias edges. Then insert a fabric strip cut on the straight of the grain to avoid problems with stretching.

As an additional precaution against stretching, use spray starch prior to piecing. Press carefully, making sure to lift your iron before moving it. (Do not iron

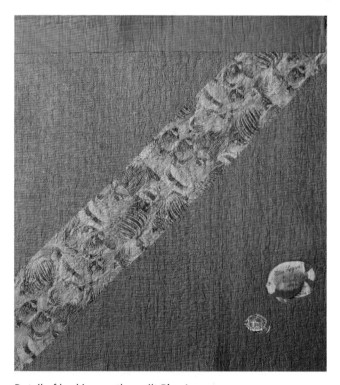

Detail of backing on the quilt **Blue Lagoon.**

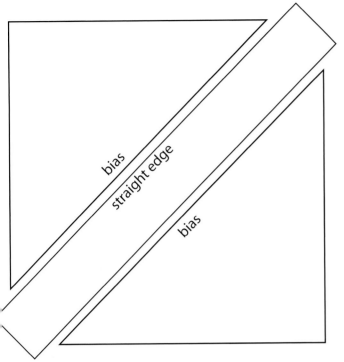

back and forth!) Your backing has grown horizontally and vertically, and is now ready to use.

WHERE, WHAT, AND HOW MUCH TO QUILT

After sandwiching your quilt (hopefully with the help of a few buddies), it's time to decide what quilting design you're going to use and whether you'll quilt by hand or by machine.

Quilts like the ones in this book, which are constructed of many small pieces, have lots of seams to contend with. This can make hand-quilting a bit more labor-intensive than usual.

Xian Hé (curved diamond) 88" x 59"
Vicki Carlson, Fort Collins, Colorado 2001

If you find hand-quilting a bit daunting, you may want to use your sewing machine instead. As for my favorite machines, the Janome Memory Craft 11000 and Professional Memory Craft 6600P were made for machine quilting. It has opened up a whole new world for me. The large 9-inch opening and the many features, make machine quilting a snap. In the past, I only hand-quilted my quilts; but I must say I love the freedom that free-motion machine quilting gives me. I can draw designs on my quilt tops with my machine quilting as if I were using a pencil, or I can needle-paint my appliqués in place.

As for what you're going to quilt, I find that an overall design is often very appealing.

Take a look at **_Java Revisited_** on page 37, and you'll see that the entire piece was hand-quilted with not just one overall design, but four! Starting at the bottom, I worked my way toward the top, changing designs along the way, and marking as I went along.

In **_Northern Exposure_** I hand-quilted using an overall design I call loop-to-loop, adding beading as I went along. It was a time-consuming process, but a very rewarding one. If machine quilting is desired, just about anything goes.

Sometimes, you may want to emphasize the shapes, as seen in the detail of **_Sandhill Cranes of Nebraska_** on page 49. To quilt and stay within the perimeters of the shapes, you can create the sense of motion.

Butterflies Are Free
(curved diamond) 37" x 40"
Louisa Smith, Loveland, CO
1994

Sometimes, not paying any attention to the shapes and simply quilting lines is very effective. Better yet, you can create double lines, as also seen here in the as seen in the detail of **Sandhill Cranes of Nebraska**. As I mentioned earlier, I travel with my quilts, and they get a lot more folding, handling, and re-folding than the average piece. So, I usually quilt them quite heavily to prevent them from wrinkling.

Your own quilts might not need quite as much quilting as the ones you see in this book. That's perfectly fine; it's all a matter of personal preference.

If you're usually a "strictly in the ditch" quilter or if you tend to cover every last square inch of every quilt with a meandering stipple you may want to expand your quilting repertoire.

For some additional inspiration, check out all the quilts in this book, which include a variety of, techniques ranging from simple parallel lines, to outlined shapes, to overall quilting motifs.

Think too about using an assortment of the colored and multi-colored threads available from Sulky,® instead of using just a single color. When I'm not quite sure which color to select, I often choose a multi-

Detail of quilting on the quilt **Sandhill Cranes of Nebraska**.

colored thread instead. It not only adds interest; it frequently works better with the multi-colored fabrics I combine in my quilts. And as an added bonus, I can often use multi-colored thread in a larger area than I could any single color so I don't have to change thread as often. The Sulky® Blendables are a favorite of mine and I must say they have an incredible line of colors available.

On page 64 I have provided some examples of overall quilting designs I particularly enjoy using. I hope you'll take advantage of some of them—and also explore some of the many good books written about machine quilting before embarking on your next project.

For inspiration I suggest you look at some favorite books of mine, written by Kathy Sandbach*.

* See Resources.

Wind Dancer (half clamshell) 51" x 51"
Joan E. Rossi, Fort Collins, CO 2004

A Few Words On Marking And Batting

My favorite marking tool is the white Clover's Chaco Liner,® which looks like a lipstick with a small serrated wheel in the tip, and contains marking powder inside. I don't recommend using colors other than white, as other quilters have reported negative experiences with them. (On one quilt, colored chalk was still visible long after the quilting was completed.) I mark only a small section at a time, and then quilt it immediately, because the white markings disappear quickly.

For hand quilting, I would recommend a bat that is easy to needle. Today, there are many options, such as the silk battings, and let us not forget the wool battings. Check with your local quilt store and see what they have to offer.

For machine quilting on the other hand, my favorite product is Quilters Dream Cotton.® This cotton batting comes in four different lofts, and I prefer Select,® the second thinnest one. The cotton batting by Warm and Natural® is another excellent choice.

TRADITIONAL BINDING OR ARTIST BINDING.

Traditional binding usually will add another edge to your quilts. Quite often, I do not want to see another edge. I then prefer to create an Artist Binding, which means the binding gets pulled all the way to the back of the quilt and is not visible from the front. I have an easy and fool proof way to accomplish this.

For example, your quilt measures 40 inches by 37 inches, cut two strips that measure 40 inches by 1-¾ inches and another two strips that measure 37 inches by 1-¾ inches. Your next step is the mark the longer strips with the 45 degree mark on your Quilter's ruler as follows; see diagram.

Then, sew the frame for your binding by mitering the strips; see below.

Place the completed frame on top of your completed and quilted top, sew all around ¼ inch from the unfinished edges. Trim the corners and turn all the way to the back of your quilt. You may want to press the edges before hand sewing the artist binding to the back of your quilt. I really hope you find this way of mitered corners on an artist binding a great and easy way to finish off your wonderful art quilts.

Lisa and I enjoy making and teaching these **One-Patch Plus** quilts. We hope we have inspired you by giving you many examples and ideas to create your own masterpieces. We hope you are motivated to continue this journey of color, design and theme. Keep us posted; we love hearing from you.

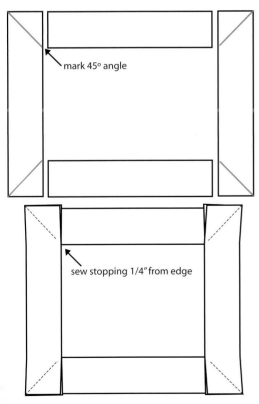

mark 45° angle

sew stopping 1/4" from edge

Mitering your border strips.

* See Resources.

THE CURVED KITE

COLOR

This wonderful photograph was the color source.

FABRICS

Choose lots of fabrics ranging from light to dark, that will color coordinate with your picture. In this case we used two color families, brown and green. These can be ¼ yard pieces or fat quarters. We have used about 45 browns and about 43 greens.

DESIGN *Curved Kite Template*

Cut three curved kite shapes from all your fabrics to get started. You will be able to add to that amount when needed.

Start "playing" on the design wall with all the cut shapes. Give yourself time and play as long as you want until you are happy with your composition. See how we designed our quilt *"Indian Paintbrush"* by looking at the photograph. I usually do NOT copy the design of a picture but rather take the color and create my own design. Melody Randol designed this quilt by referring to her photograph. Either way will work.

SEWING

Take three pieces off the design wall and sew them together (refer to figure 6 on page 30) creating half of the hexagonal shapes you will end up with; see photograph. Notice the pressing, which is always in one direction, creating a flower-like center. When pinning remember to keep the belly on the bottom and the bite on the top! Place them back on the design wall in the correct space. Do this to all the appropriate pieces and press. Continue to construct the quilt top by sewing these shapes into rows as shown in the photograph. Give it one more pressing.

Creating the hexagonal shapes.

Indian Paintbrush (curved kite) 45" x 35"
Melody Randol, Loveland, Colorado 2007

Because this curved kite shape creates edges that are also curved, you have the option of leaving them as is, adding borders or just simply cutting them off. We used straight edges, placing our quilt top on our cutting table and with the use of a quilters rule and rotary cutter, we simply cut the curves off.

Creating rows from the hexagonal shapes.

Ready for the embellishing?

EMBELLISHING

In this particular quilt we have chosen to enhance with free motion embroidery. The Indian paintbrush images were heavily free motion machine embroidered using a lot of threads in various colors. You may opt for other embellishing methods, see chapter 7.

Complete your embellishing and quilt as desired. Add a binding of your choice. You have now finished your masterpiece.

The Half Clamshell

Color

We used a piece of fabric as a color source, about 2 yards.

Fabrics

Consider selecting approximately 40 fabrics ranging from light to dark, that color-coordinate with your source fabric. These can be ¼ yard pieces or fat quarters. Please refer to the focus fabric and note the background in this fabric is black. We have opted NOT to use the black, but elected to use dark purple as our darkest fabric used.

Design *The Half Clamshell Template*

Remember this shape, can be cut regular or reversed. The added bonus of using batik fabrics is, that one can cut out the shape and use it either way. Lots of batik fabrics were used in this quilt.

Cut three half clamshell shapes from all your fabrics to get started. You will be able to add or subtract to that amount when needed.

You are now ready to start "playing" on the design wall with all the cut shapes. I suggest you start with your light colored fabrics as in this composition the light section is quite large. Gradually you could go into medium with your dark fabrics more towards the bottom and right side of this composition.

Give yourself time to "play" as long as you want until you are happy with your composition. Refer to the quilt "Papillion" for help in placement.

Sewing

Start by sewing all the straight seams first. Take two pieces off the wall sew the straight seams, then press them open and place them back on the design wall. Once you have sewed all the straight seams (see figure 11 page 32), you can move on to sewing the curved seams. Take the curved seam pieces you want to sew off the design wall making sure the belly is on the bottom and the bite is on top. Press the curved seams only when you have an area where they all meet, so that you can press them into that flower-like center (see figure 5 page 30). Continue to construct the quilt top, and give it one more pressing on the right side. The color and design are done. Ready for the embellishing?

EMBELLISHING

In this case we used *Steam-A-Seam Lite II* and adhered it to the back of a piece of our focus fabric. We then carefully cut out as many flowers and butterflies as we thought we may need, placed them on the quilt and pressed them in place.

We opted to quilt the embellishing on. That simply means, we sandwiched the quilt, batting and backing with one inch safety pins and as we were doing our machine quilting, we proceeded with free-motion embroidery, (through all three layers) to secure the flowers in place. See chapter 7 for more details on this procedure.

Add an Artist binding (page 51) and you have completed your wonderful project.

Don't forget the hanging sleeve and label!

Papillion (half clamshell) 45" x 28"
Vicki Carlson, Fort Collins, Colorado 2007

Project 3
The Flowing Ribbon

Before starting this project, we need to explain that the flowing ribbon template is actually two half clamshell shapes, side by side. Two of these flowing ribbon shapes create your 6" block for this project. I particularly like this shape, because it is an excellent tool to show off the fabric, especially when you are telling a story. By that I mean we often are attracted to a piece of fabric, which tells a story. The piece may be a scene of one of Monet's paintings, or it may be a landscape, that shows off a farm scene or it could be an underwater scene. The piece of fabric for this project was just such a fabric. See fabric selection.

Calypso Cascade (flowing ribbon) 39" x 34"
Melody Randol, Loveland, Colorado 2007

COLOR

In this case the color source was this incredibly interesting fabric, and we started with about 2 yards. This fabric is also your theme; see fabric selection.

FABRIC

Select approximately 10 fabrics ranging from light to dark, that will color coordinate with your source fabric. These can be ¼ yard pieces or fat quarters. See photograph of fabrics used.

DESIGN *The Flowing Ribbon Template*

Before cutting your pieces consider a few important facts about this shape. We have already stated that two flowing ribbon shapes sewed together will form your 6-inch finished block. If you select to turn your template over, and you cut a reversed or mirror image piece,

reversed block

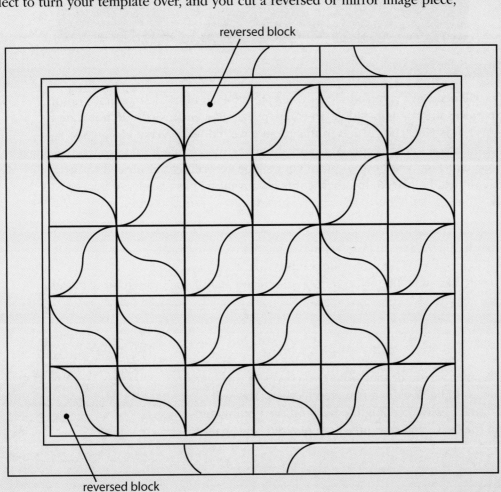

reversed block

project 3: The Flowing Ribbon project

Playing with pieces on the design wall.

remember that you will need two reversed pieces to create a 6-inch block. I sometimes opt to not use the reverse pieces in my composition. To create puzzle-like shapes you do not want to turn the template over. It is your choice, and in this project we did use reverse pieces. See layout of quilt and cut the shapes accordingly. You also should be aware that if you are working with a fabric that has direction, you need to place your shape accordingly. You need to know where in your design it will be placed. In other words if your fabric has people on it as we have here, you need to make sure they don't appear upside down and side ways.

Play with your pieces on the design wall until you have a wonderful composition. See diagram on page 57 for easy placement. Please note: using somewhat of a contrast between shapes, will result in more distinct curved lines in your composition. Using less contrast will result in an illusion of curves. Play with the placement of your shapes until you are happy with the composition.

SEWING

Ready to sew? Remember we are dealing with two curves in this block. The construction needs to be done in a two step method. You will sew one curve at a time, always keeping the belly on the bottom and the bite on top. Pin the curve and sew, turn over pin and sew again to

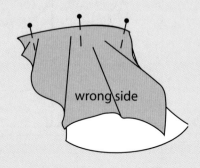

wrong side

complete the block (page 30). In this project we are sewing from the middle to the outside edge. The tail end of the shape is always on top! If you use a batik fabric (because of the tight weave), you may have to pull on that tail end a bit to make it stretch just a little to make the curve smooth. Turn the piece over and do it again, starting in the middle and sewing to the outside edge to complete your block. When pressing the piece, always press away from the outer edge, so that you can see the seam allowance better (figure 5, page 30). Notice the seam in the center of the block; it changes direction!

Take one block off the wall at one time, sew it, press it and place it back in the same space. Construct all your blocks, and sew these blocks to each other to create rows. You can now press the seams open from block to block, for less bulk. We have added a small inner border, cut 1 ¼ inch wide, to contain the image and then added an outer border (cut 2 inches wide) to complete the quilt top. Notice, in some places we mimicked the composition's design and continued that into the border. Your quilt top is completed.

EMBELLISHING

Because we used a fabric for our theme, we really do not need to embellish. It is up to you to make that decision, depending on your fabric choices. As you can see in this quilt we have cut some of the images from our source fabric and added it to the quilt top. See chapter 7 for other embellishing procedures.

Quilt as desired, and add a binding of your choice. Create a hanging sleeve and a wonderful label. Your project is completed. Congratulations!

THE CURVED DIAMOND

COLOR

A piece of fabric as a color source, about 1 yard.

FABRICS

Approximately 22 fabrics ranging from light to dark, that color-coordinate with your source fabric. These can be ¼ yard pieces or fat quarters. Seven or less of these fabrics need to be about ½ yard pieces, for possible use in the borders. Look at the framed border on this project to give you some help in selecting fabrics.

DESIGN *Curved Diamond Template*

Cut three curved diamond shapes from all your fabrics to get started, you can add to that later if needed. You will also need to cut some 3" and 4" wide strips to piece to each other, so that you can cut additional shapes. See page 32.

You are now ready to start "playing" on the design wall with all the cut shapes. Do this until you are happy with your composition. Refer to the quilt **"Summer Bouquet"** and the quilt's diagram on page 63 for help in placement.

SEWING

Take three pieces off the design wall and sew them together (see figure 6, page 30), creating the curved hexagonal shapes. Press the seam in the same direc-

Summer Bouquet (curved diamond) 43" x 42"
Louisa Smith, Loveland, Colorado 2007

tion, creating a flower-like center, (figure 5, page 30). And place them back on the design wall in the correct space. Do this to all the appropriate pieces and press. Continue to construct the quilt top and give it one more pressing.

The Borders:

Depending on your color scheme and fabrics chosen, select the fabrics you want to use in your borders. Cut 6 ½" wide strips from these selected fabrics. This could vary from 1 to 7 or more fabrics, it is your choice.

To measure your quilt for the borders, refer to page 35 and measure from the most inward points to establish the width and length. For the quilt *"Summer Bouquet"* this was: 33 ½ inches by 35 ½ inches.

Take an additional 1 ½" off both measurements, which will be: 32 inches by 34 inches. This measurement is you're inside frame measurement and you will need to add 12" (twice your finished border size 2 x 6" = 12") so my outside frame measurements are: 44 inches by 46 inches.

You need to construct the left and the right border, to measure exactly 44", and you will need to construct both the top and the bottom borders, to measure exactly 46". Piece if needed.

Miter them inwards and you have created the frame as seen in the photograph that will measure exactly 44 inches by 46 inches on the outside edge.

Place your quilt on top of the framed border and appliqué your quilt in place, either by hand or by machine. You have now completed the first two steps, color and design. Ready for the embellishing?

EMBELLISHING

In this particular quilt we have chosen to enhance with hand appliqué and since our color source was a piece of fabric, we used several leaves and floral images, and cut them out. Making sure we had about ¼" seam allowance around all the images used. One of our border fabrics was a floral as well and we also cut some images from that fabric. We created a floral bouquet and after auditioning it on our design wall, we hand appliquéed it in place. You may opt for other embellishing methods , see chapter 7.

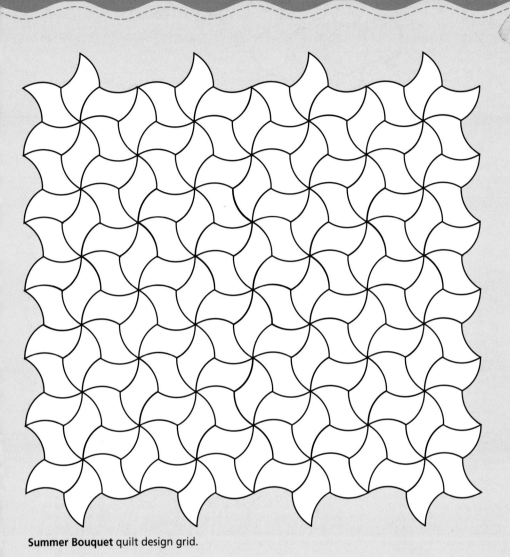

Summer Bouquet quilt design grid.

pebbles

curlie

swirls

linear

leaves

double leaves

flowers

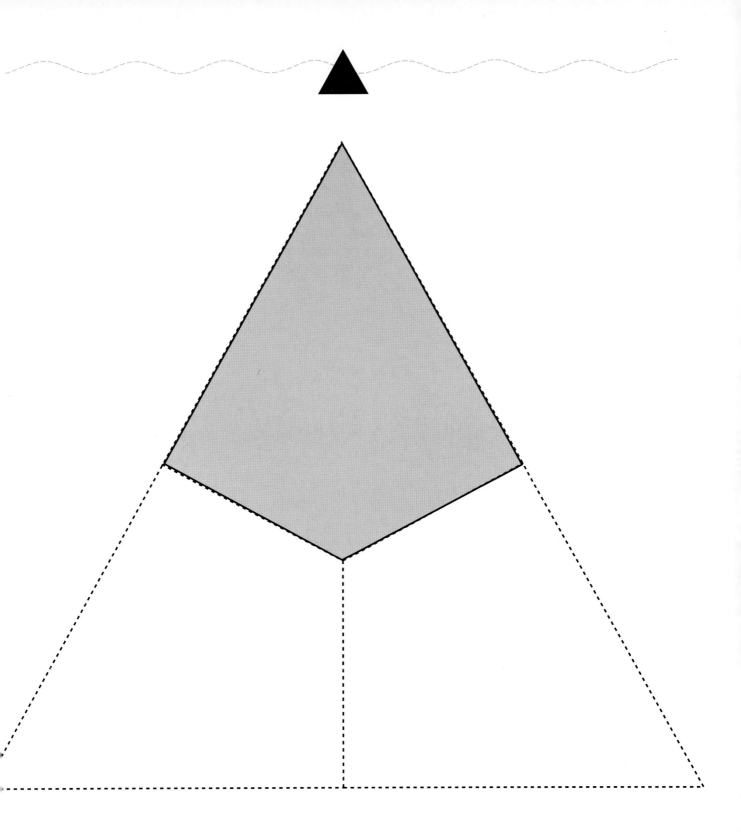

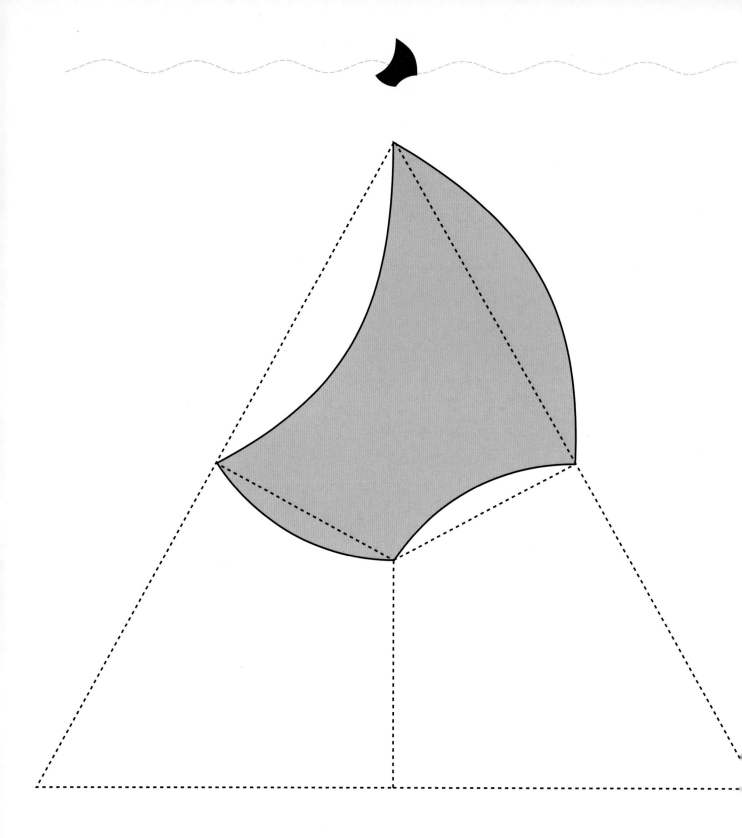

CURVED KITE TEMPLATE

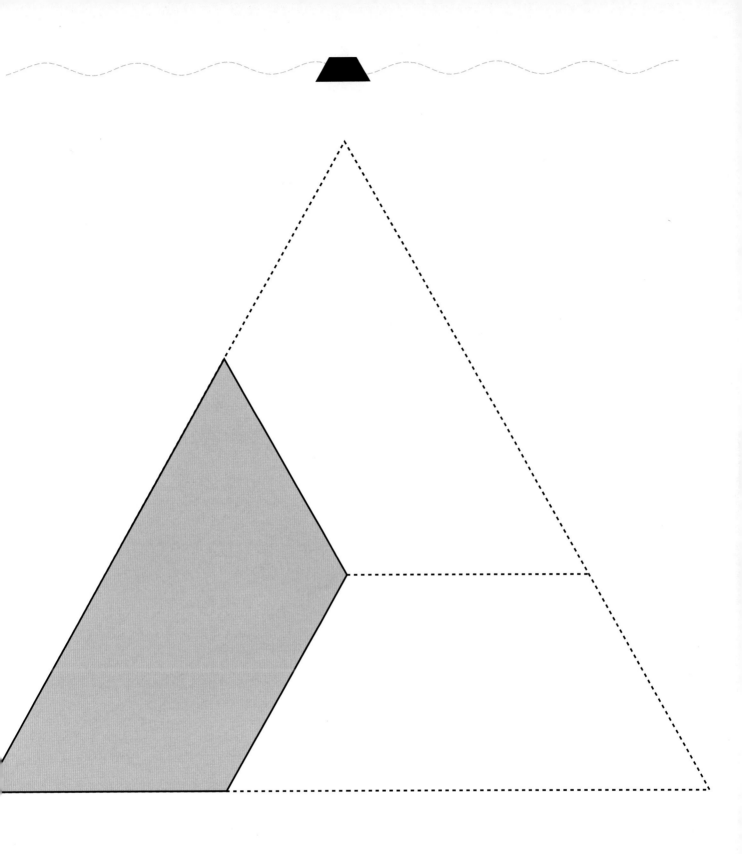

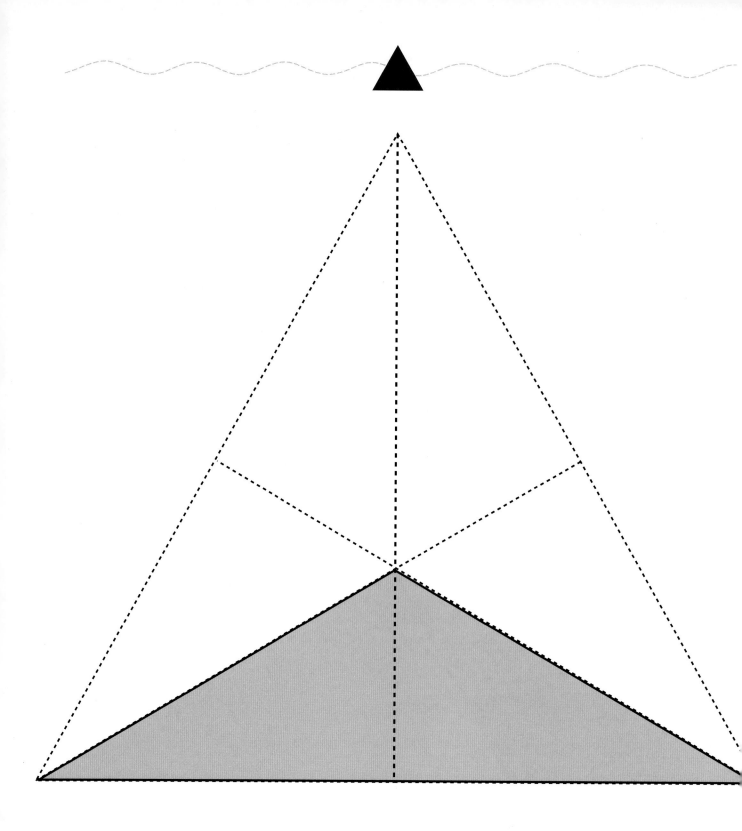

ISOSCELES TRIANGLE TEMPLATES

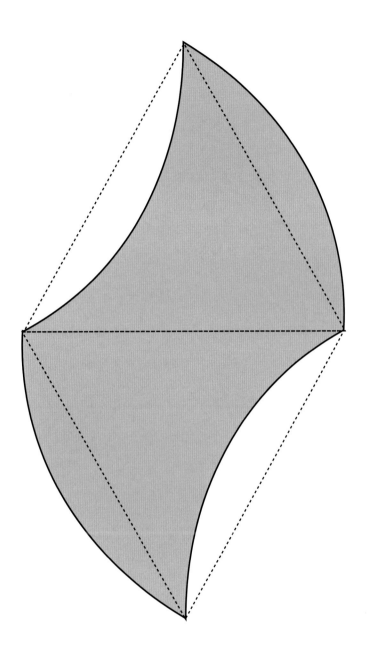

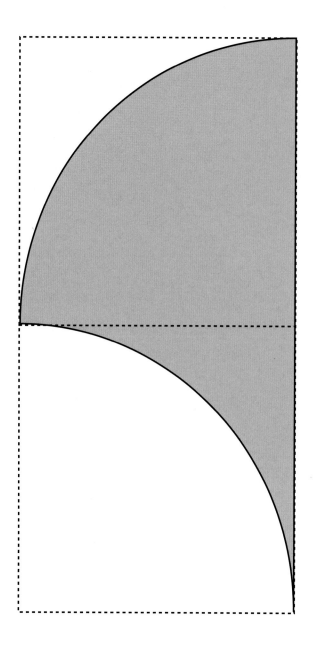

HALF CLAMSHELL TEMPLATE

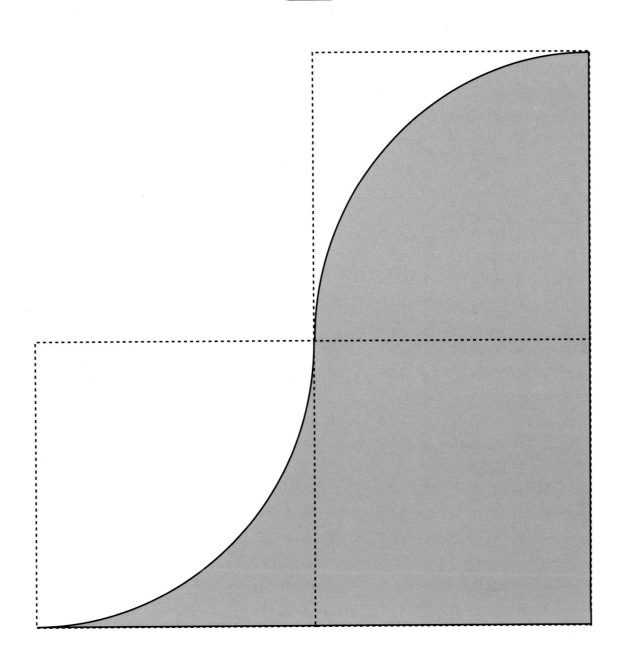

KITE GRID

HALF HEXAGON GRID

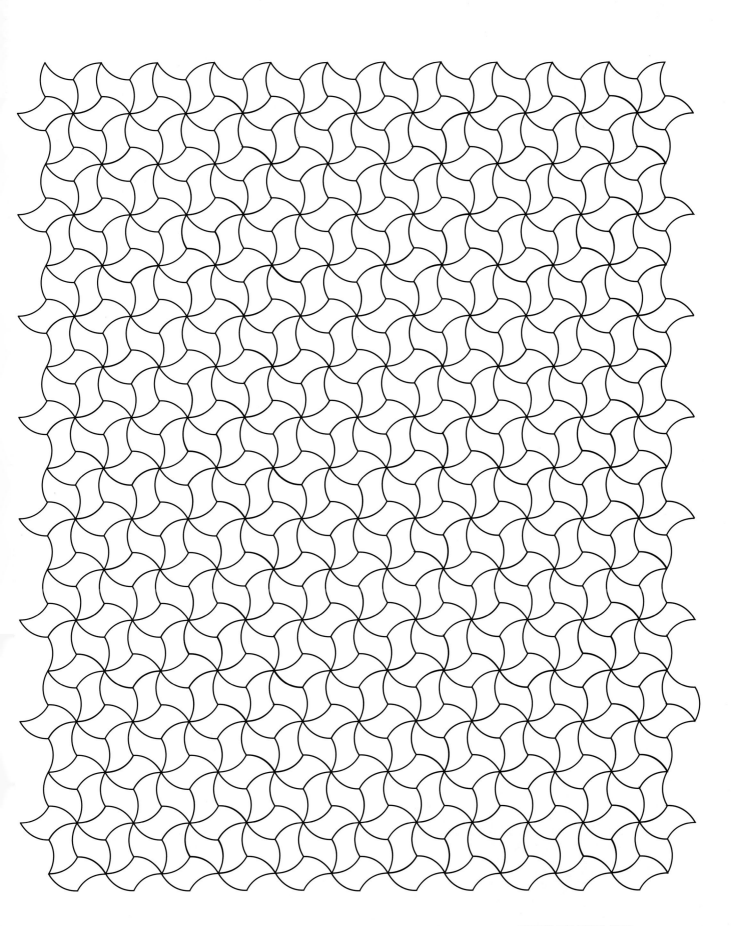

RESOURCES

Ardco Precision Metal Non-Skid Quilt templates

QuiltSmith, Ltd.
252 Cedar Rd.
Poquoson, VA 23662
1-800-982-7326
757-868-7326
Fax: 757-868-3866
www.ardcotemplates.com

Chaco Liner

Clover Needlecraft, Inc.
13438 Alondra Blvd.
Cerritos, CA 90703-2315
562-282-0200
www.clover-usa.com

Rotary cutters: RTY-1/G—28mm and RTY-4-18mm

Charlie's "E-Z" Mat Cutters and all "OLFA" products
www.matandquiltcutters.com
1-800-735-8656

Rotary mat: RM-12S

Charlie's "E-Z" Mat Cutters and all "OLFA" products
www.matandquiltcutters.com
1-800-735-8656

Curve Master Presser Foot (for sewing curves without pinning)

Just Curves
2549B Eastbluff Dr. #123
Newport Beach, CA 92660
949-721-0865
www.justcurves.biz

Janome Memory Craft 11000 and Professional Memory Craft 6600

Janome-America, Inc.
10 Industrial Ave.
Mahwah, NJ 07430
1-800-631-0183
www.janome.com

One Patch Plus templates See-through acrylic templates, marked with ¼" seam allowances, plus lines for strip piecing.

Quilt Escapes, LLC
4821 14th St. SW
Loveland, CO 80537
970-593-1265
Fax: 970-593-1378
www.quiltescapes.com

Quilting Books

C& T Publishing, Inc.
P.O. Box 1456
Lafayette, CA 94549
1-800-284-1114
www.ctpub.com

Quilters Dream Cotton Batting—Select

Quilters Dream Batting
589 Central Dr.
Virginia Beach, VA 23454
1-800-626-8866
www.quiltersdreambatting.com

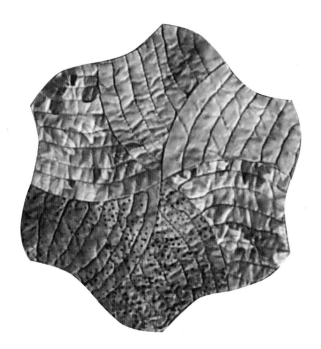

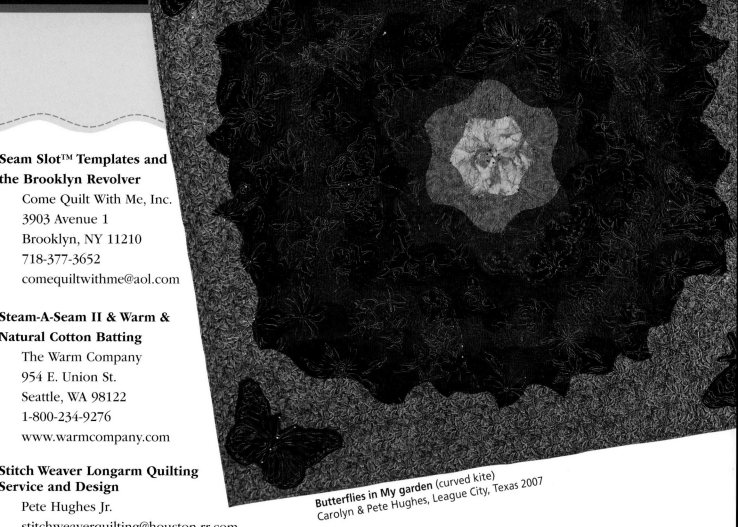

Butterflies in My garden (curved kite)
Carolyn & Pete Hughes, League City, Texas 2007

Seam Slot™ Templates and the Brooklyn Revolver

Come Quilt With Me, Inc.
3903 Avenue 1
Brooklyn, NY 11210
718-377-3652
comequiltwithme@aol.com

Steam-A-Seam II & Warm & Natural Cotton Batting

The Warm Company
954 E. Union St.
Seattle, WA 98122
1-800-234-9276
www.warmcompany.com

Stitch Weaver Longarm Quilting Service and Design

Pete Hughes Jr.
stitchweaverquilting@houston.rr.com

Sulky® threads

Sulky® of America, Inc.
PO Box 494129
Port Charlotte, FL 33949-4129
www.Sulky.com

Speed Stitch, Inc
2298 Vale Lake Dr.
York, SC 29745
Phone: 866-829-7235
Fax: 803-985-3106
www.speedstitch.com
or info@speedstitch.com

Uncommon Thread, Inc.
Box 338 S. Sharon Amity Rd.
Charlotte, NC 28211
877-294-5427
www.uncommonthread.com

teachers

Louisa Smith
author, lecturer, and teacher
4821 14th Street SW
Loveland, CO 80537
970-593-1265
www.quiltescapes.com

Lisa Harris
author and teacher
4821 14th Street SW
Loveland, CO 80537
970-593-1265
www.Quiltescapes.com

Carol Wight Jones
lecturer and teacher
2964 Brittany Place
Anchorage, AK 99504
970-646-9922
Email: CWJQUILTER@aol.com

Anita Shackleford
author, lecturer and teacher
Thimbleworks
PO Box 462
Bucyrus, OH 44820
www.thimbleworks.com

Ann Fahl
author, lecturer and teacher
5033 Deerwood Drive
Racine, WI 53406-2305
www.AnnFahl.com

Kathy Sandbach
author, lecturer and teacher.
www.machinequiltlady.com

About the Authors

Louisa L. Smith

Louisa was born in Indonesia and educated in the Netherlands, and she came to the United States in 1960. Although her quilting started with a traditional approach, soon new and exciting designs took over, and the traditional gave way to more innovative work. The incredible flexibility that fiber offers attracted her to "paint" with fabrics. She enjoys collaborating on new designs with her daughter, Lisa, a graphic artist who shares her mothers love of quilting. Louisa resides in Loveland, Colorado, with her husband and mother. This is Louisa's third book.

Lisa Harris

Growing up with a Mom who quilted Lisa, learned to sew at a very young age. Sewing clothing was her first passion, however watching her mother grow as a quilter she saw an opportunity for her creativity in quilting. Always creative, Lisa graduated from Rhode Island School of Design with degree in graphic design. As an art director for more than 20 years, she saw quilting as an outlet for her creativity away from work. Often collaborating with her Mom on designs she is constantly looking for new ways to push the boundaries of "quilting". Lisa resides in Johnstown, Colorado with her husband Brian, and dog Shadow.

CHECK OUT ALL THE TEMPLATE SETS AVAILABLE FROM QUILTESCAPES!

9" BASIC TEMPLATE SET
$29.95

9" BASIC SET II
$24.95

ADVANCED TEMPLATE SET
$49.95

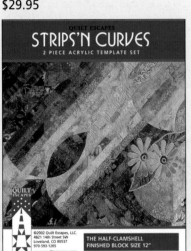

12" HALF-CLAMSHELL SET
$17.95

9" NEGATIVE/POSITIVE SET
$29.95

9" SWIRL SET
$25.95

8" FLOWING RIBBON TEMPLATE SET
$9.95

6" FLOWING RIBBON TEMPLATE SET
$6.95

6" MINI BEG 'N BORROW SET
$24.95

ONE-PATCH PLUS 4-PIECE TEMPLATE SET $24.95

CALL 1-970-593-1265
or order online at www.quiltescapes.com

Quilt Escapes, LLC 4821 14th Street SW, Loveland, Colorado 80537

OTHER BOOKS BY LOUISA SMITH

Available from C&T Publishing

ISBN: 1-57120-168-8
Description: 96p, color
UPC: 734817-102557
Price: $23.95

Get ready for Louisa Smith's innovative new quiltmaking technique, and see basic strip piecing in a whole new light. The combination of straight lines and gentle curves creates zingy but easy-to-make quilts. You'll be hooked before you know it!

• 3 complete quilt projects to lead you from beginner through advanced levels
• Learn to choose colors and lay out blocks to give your quilt drama and contrast
• Louisa teaches you to draft your own curved templates, or you can use readily available commercial ones
• Create one-of-a-kind quilts that look complicated but are simple to construct

Janet Jo Smith, Quilters Newsletter Magazine
September 1, 2002
The joy of strip piecing is that it can make simple pieced blocks look rich and complex. This book reveals Louisa's talent for combining complementary fabric strips to make beautiful yardage from which she cuts curved patches to piece blocks. The combination of linear strips and curved shapes creates some unique and interesting quilts.

Fabrications
October 1, 2002
Louisa Smith's guide to her fresh new form of strip piecing is actually the epitome of style and taste. This is a well-produced guide to an easy and fun method that will give you free reign to experiment and approach strip piecing from a whole new angle.

Art You WeaR
September 1, 2003
Give me a variation on strip piecing and I'm there! It's my favorite way to create new fabric.

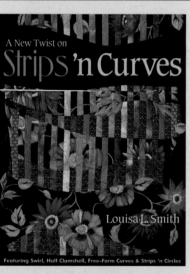

ISBN: 1-57120-396-6
Description: 88p, color
UPC: 734817-105060
Price: $26.95

Strip Piecing With Twists and Turns!

• Start with basic strip piecing, add easy and gently curved edges, and prepare to be amazed!
• Louisa introduces 4 design concepts, 2 template based and 2 template free, all with step-by-step instructions

Whether you own Louisa's 2001 best-selling Strips 'n Curves or you're new to the world of combining curved-edge and strip piecing, you'll love the fresh ideas and fabulous inspiration in this book. Learn Louisa's four new techniques (Half Clamshell, Free-Form Curves, Strips 'n Circles, and The Swirl); then try them in four complete project quilts! Lots of step-by-step photos and clear instructions ensure your success. Ideas for home décor, garments, and quilts, quilts, quilts!

Quilter's Newsletter Magazine
November 1, 2007
"Louisa L. Smith's second book on strips and curves applies the basic concept of string piecing—creating "strata" of pieced strips—to more complicated patchwork. Make half clamshell blocks and learn to piece "the swirl." Cut the blocks using the templates provided and reassemble them for dynamic, innovative designs. With all this piecing, cutting, and resewing, your top is bound to be out of shape. Louisa's tip for squaring up before applying the borders or binding is worth remembering."

New Zealand Quilter
October 1, 2007
"Curves are popular with quilters and Louisa Smith's new book follows on from her best-seller Strips 'n Curves. The technique is used for everything from quilts to fashion garments. Aimed at the confident beginner through to intermediate level quilters, the step-by-step photos make the concepts easy to grasp. Clear instructions lead you through from basic strip piecing for the base fabric to cutting the curves and creating your new design. You can use the technique free-form for flowing organic designs, or with templates for a more geometric effect. Combined with traditional blocks such as New York Beauty, you can achieve a complex design quite simply."

C&T Publishing, Inc.• 1651 Challenge Drive, Concord, CA 94520-5206
Online: www.ctpub.com or e-mail: ctinfo@ctpub.com
Phone: (800) 284-1114 toll-free in U.S.• (925) 677-0377 International · Fax (925) 677-0373